Parenting Toddlers: A Complete Guide for Raising Disciplined, Happier, and Confident Kids

Trista Frost

Table of Contents

Introduction

Congratulations on purchasing this book.

Being a parent is never an easy task. Raising children who are happy, confident, and healthy, both physically and mentally, is one of the most demanding tasks a person can be faced with. There are numerous challenges parents face at every nook and corner of parenting that they cannot run away from but are required to face head-on.

Although parenting is quite a serious matter, most parents do not approach it with measurable seriousness, which leads to issues, misunderstandings, and intense distress in the relationship between parents and children.

So what can you do to avoid this from happening to you and your family? What steps can you take to ensure that your children live up to their fullest potential with your guidance and support? What points do you need to keep in mind to avoid ruining your relationship with your child?

This book will provide you with the answers to these questions and also act as a guiding tool to guarantee that you can nurture your child well. With the tips provided in this book, you will be able to develop a healthy relationship with your child, understand their needs, and effectively communicate your desires and expectations with them to lead to harmony and understanding.

What is Effective Parenting?

Before you learn about healthy relationship development, it is crucial that you understand the importance of effective parenting and why it should be a part of your routine. Being a new parent is undoubtedly full of difficulties and challenges, but it gets easier for you if you know how to work around them.

So what exactly is good parenting or effective parenting? It is the parenting style that involves taking into consideration your child's age and development stage. It revolves around maintaining age-appropriate expectations from your child and enforcing suitable discipline-building and socializing strategies.

The good that effective parenting brings is that it helps children develop independence and provides for their need for support and understanding in a way that is best for them.

In doing so, children learn that they can rely on their parents for whatever problems they may be facing or will face in the future, which gives them a sense of belonging and provides them with a safe place. With effective parenting, children develop a growth mindset instead of a fixed mindset, which helps them grow as individuals later in life.

Why is a Healthy Parent-Child Relationship Important?

The bond shared between parents and children is one of purity and unconditional love. Parenting can surely be one of the most difficult tasks, but it is also one of the most fulfilling ones. Watching your child grow into their adulthood and inculcating all the good habits and behaviors that you spent years trying to develop in them can be very emotionally fulfilling to watch.

What makes a parent-child relationship so important is that it is the basic foundation on which a child's growth depends. Suppose a child's relationship with his or her parent is not ideal or is unhealthy to a certain extent. In that case, it affects the child negatively in many ways, which generally show up when the child has grown into an adult. This is the reason why we find so many adults stuck in toxic situations because they mimic their childhood environment. Breaking these unhealthy patterns often requires therapy or counseling.

A healthy parent-child relationship is one where the child has his or her needs met and nurtured. These needs can be physical, emotional as well as social. Positive parenting makes sure that a child is not left alone to defend his needs and wants in any situation unless it is for his or her benefit or learning. How a child is raised, and the amount of support and guidance experienced by the child goes on to be the foundation of a child's personality and also affects his mental, physical and emotional well-being.

Children who have a healthy parent-child relationship experience an upper hand over those who grow up without one. Because such children have a strong connection to their parents and have the fulfillment of having their needs met by their caregivers, they stand a better chance of developing happy relationships with others in the future as well. Children who grow up having an unhealthy relationship with their parents often experience difficulty in maintaining healthy relationships with others as they mature into adulthood.

This is why the quality of relationship you have with your child is vital because it affects a considerable part of your child's well-being, thereby influencing the quality of life your child leads in the future. This is why you should be mindful of your parenting techniques and how effective they are towards nurturing your child's growth and developing the required qualities of a good human being.

What Does Effective Parenting Require?

As per most research conducted on parenting styles, it has been found that the best parenting style is an authoritative style. An authoritative parenting style is one where there is a balance or equilibrium between nurturing your child and being firm with him or her when it is required. It has been seen that when children are subjected to an authoritative parenting style, the outcomes are generally best for them in terms of physical and mental well-being and academic success.

While parenting style can be a very personal thing and depends on what works best for your child, there is another thing that determines how well your relationship with your child is going to be. The most important thing that you should keep in mind when it comes to raising a child is that no amount of effective parenting is going to help build a healthy relationship with your child if it is not backed with consistency and routine. Forming a habit can be difficult, but it is going to be worth it when you start seeing the positive effects it brings towards nurturing and bringing up your child.

Some of the basic things which are common in all parenting styles are having loving and warm interactions with your children for you to build a connection with them and for them to feel safe and protected in your presence.

Where Should You Start?

You may have heard the saying, "Charity begins at home," and although good parenting starts at home, it initially begins with you changing aspects of yourself that you would hate to see developing in your child. For instance, if you want your children to be punctual, you have to start by being punctual yourself. Children do not hear as much as they watch and imitate us.

To be a good parent, you first need to be a good human. The qualities you want to see in your child should be the qualities you can see in yourself. Otherwise, you will just be pushing your child to achieve a goal that you lack the knowledge of achieving and cannot guide your child through. This will not only be unfair to your child, but by looking at how you perform the said task, they may feel like they are trying to achieve something which is not possible to achieve.

You must realize that parenting is not only a difficult task because you are required to feed and look after a child for years, but also because it challenges you to be the best possible version of yourself, which is not possible unless you are truly dedicated to giving your child the best childhood you can.

Some parents do not take the responsibility of parenting seriously, and it manifests in broken homes and emotionally torn children. If a person's childhood is unhappy, it is most likely that the unhappiness follows them for the rest of their lives. Parents who are unable to provide their child with the required love and affection they need either are unaware of the consequences it may have on the child later in the future or are too reluctant to put in the efforts to change their habits and patterns.

Reflecting on your childhood may give you a general idea of how you want to parent your child. You may find that there are certain things that you want to do just like your parents did, just as there are other things that you want to do completely differently. The first step I want you to take before you start reading this book is to reflect within and get a basic idea of what you think your parenting technique looks like.

Do you want it to be assertive at all times? Or do you want to let your child decide everything on their own with little or no interference from your side? For now, I just want you to picture what you think is going to be best for you and your child and hold on to that idea. As you go through this book, you will see that there are techniques that you can use for better parenting, and if you find that it contradicts your opinions and beliefs, you can change those thought patterns, leaving the bad behind and moving on with the positives. Having a basic idea of what your ideal parenting looks like will make your learning easier because you may have only a handful of things to change as you read through the chapters that follow.

Once you have a child, you may know how hectic your daily schedule gets. But do not let survival mode get in the way of your parenting. Getting through the day may be one of your daily goals, but it should not hamper your parenting goals.

Remember To Take Care of Yourself Too

All that said, it is equally important that you take care of your own needs alongside those of your child. By not paying attention to your requirements and taking time out for yourself, you risk being overworked and stressed. No one can provide their best when they are stressed. Oftentimes, overburdened parents cannot devote time to their children, and even if they manage to do so, they may easily get irritated with the child's age-appropriate behaviors.

How you practice self-care will greatly impact your family life as well. Failing in this area will cause disturbances in the mind of your child as well. While it is normal for you to occasionally get angry and frustrated, it is not normal for you to project it on your child. At times when you feel overwhelmed with your emotions, try to pause and think about the effect it may have on your child if you let it out uncontrolled.

Do not let the negativity you feel inside yourself get to your child and hamper his or her growth in any way. The only way for you to successfully do this is for you to take necessary breaks and time out for yourself when you think it appropriate to do so. Also, you mustn't start neglecting yourself while trying to take care of your family's needs. You, like anyone in your life, deserve love, care, and pampering.

Final Thoughts

Whether you are a new parent or not, you may already be well aware of how important parenting is to raise a child. If you are a new parent, all this may seem overwhelming to you at first, but as you go on with this book, I promise you that it gets easier and simpler. The good thing about this is that although parenting is hard, it brings its own set of rewards that you can experience after a couple of years. If you keep in mind the points mentioned in this book, you will find yourself a guide and can venture on this path of parenthood with much more ease and knowledge. I wish you all the best in your parenting journey.

There are plenty of books on this subject on the market; thanks again for choosing this one! Every effort was made to ensure it was full of as much useful information as possible. Please enjoy!

Chapter 1: Why Do We Parent the Way We Do?

Parenting is tough. There can be no simpler or easier way to put it. It is true that a child changes a lot and believe me, nobody can be a perfect parent. You will find a lot of so call "experts" giving you a lot of advice on what you should do and how to handle your child, but remember, every child is different, and thus, you will be able to understand what works for you only through "trial and error method."

So does that mean you have got to do everything on your own? Well, no. You can take advice from people around you, but before understanding how to be a good parent, you must understand your parenting skills properly and have complete knowledge about your child.

Can you find a single person on this planet who will tell you that kids are easy to deal with? As Charles Dickens wrote in his book, A Tale of Two Cities, "It was the best times, it was the worst times" this phrase describes parenting in the best way possible. There are times when you feel wonderful to be a parent, but there are times when every parent feels miserable as well.

That is exactly why you must know the basics of parenting, understand your parenting techniques, and understand your child's psychology before reacting or responding to them. In this chapter, I will discuss all such topics and help you embrace the best parts of parenting and help you get through the worst phases.

Understand the Psychology Behind Parenting

So, where do you learn parenting from? There is no such school or course that you can take before becoming a parent, so where do you learn it from? Sure, you can read some books and take advice from people around you, but most of your parenting skills come naturally or from your instinct.

Well, that does not mean it is a bad thing. Rather, it means that you should take some time and try to understand what affects the way you are parenting – is it the way your parents have treated you? Or is it the way you always wanted your parents to treat you? To become a better parent, you must understand what experiences in your life influences your parenting skills.

Here is a list of things that might have influenced your role as a parent and must help you understand why you parent the way you do –

The way your parents treated you –

Well, the influence that our parents or people who raised us have on us is undoubtedly the strongest. And it is not something unnatural. You have been influenced by them and have first-hand experience of their parenting skills for several years, which will impact the kind of parent you are.

At times, you must have found yourself reacting to situations in a similar way your parents did; it can be scolding your kid or even pampering them. As mentioned earlier, it is not always bad; you must have learned some great things from your parents as well.

For example, my parents never spoke ill about anyone in the family in front of me; sure, they had their issues, but that never reached my ear when I was young, and that is exactly what I have been doing as well.

The way your parents didn't treat you but ideally should have –

Just like our parents teach us a lot about what we must do as parents, sadly, they also teach us a lot of things that we must not do when we are parents. In fact, some children even grow up promising never to be like their parents.

For example, your parents never had time for you or never took you out and spent quality time with you, which might have hurt you a lot as a kid. That is exactly why, now that you are a parent, you never do that. In fact, no matter what comes up, you always make time for your kid.

Your values and cultures –

A lot of our parenting techniques also depend on the values and culture we have been raised in. For example, if you have been raised in a culture where showing physical affection is not a thing, you might not be able to show that to your kid as well.

In fact, that is the case with corporal punishment as well. There are a lot of places in this world where hitting your child is considered normal as a form of punishment, so parenting really depends on your culture and values.

Your personality –

 Other than all the things mentioned above, your personality also plays a great role in determining the kind of parent you will become.

For example, if you have anxiety issues, you will be very protective of your child and will keep a close eye on their activity. You will start freaking out even if they fall sick. Such personality traits can easily affect your parenting skills.

 A parent who finds it difficult to set limits in their own life will also face difficulty in setting limits for their kid's life, a parent who is not disciplined will not be able to bring the discipline in their kid's life, and that is how it works. So, try to understand your traits and do not let them affect your role as a parent, as it's not ideal.

What your kid brings out in you –

 Your children can bring out the best as well as the worst in you. You must have heard a lot of people saying that they quit smoking after their kid was born. That is the kind of positive effect your kid might have on you.

Similarly, your kid might have a negative impact on your parenting skills as well. If your kid irritates you or defies you, you might also end up reacting to them similarly. Although the reaction is quite understandable, that is not how a parent must react.

The advice you get from people around you –

 Parents are undoubtedly the ones that get a lot of advice. These advices can come from your parents, relatives, friends, and even random strangers on the streets.

Other than that, there are also a lot of parenting books available these days. Such things also influence your role as a parent.

Lastly, there is science behind parenting –

Most parents also look into scientific experiences, analyze the data and then decide which parenting technique they should use. Research studies often influence parents to understand and balance their parenting skills.

For example, some parents do not understand when they should be strict and when they should be lenient and take matters lightly. Such studies help them to determine their role in different situations better.

Of course, there can be other aspects that influence your parenting skills and child, but it is also true that your style changes from kid to kid and also a moment to moment.

Also, remember, although parenting is mostly instinctual and natural, it can also be deliberate, thoughtful, and rational with your effort.

Tips to Understand Your Child's Psychological And Emotional Development

As a parent, you have a huge impact on your child's emotional and psychological development. As a parent, it is your responsibility to understand your child's emotions and then respond to them properly.

Believe me, in order to understand this. You do not need a degree in psychology. But why do you need to understand your child? Why is it such an important part of good parenting? Being curious about your child's behavior and trying to understand their actions will help you regulate your actions.

So, here are some tips that will help you understand your child's psychology better –

Observe your child –

One of the greatest and simplest ways to learn about your kid is to observe them. Along with that, you will have to show your child that you are interested in them. Remember, each child is unique, so observe their behavior, actions, and expressions carefully.

You can also ask yourself a few questions like "what does your child like the best?" or "how long is it taking your child to get familiar with an environment?". Finding answers to these questions will help you understand your child better. But while doing so, remember not to judge them but only observe them.

Spend quality time with your child –

These days, parents are very busy with their work and often do not get enough time for their kids. But that is absolutely wrong. Parents must be great at 'multi-tasking' and will have to find out time for their kids.

If you want to understand your kid, you will have to spend quality time with them. Talk to them, make them feel that you are interested in knowing about them, and ask them how their day was.

You can also take them out for a walk and play with them. Also, remember spending quality time does not mean you will have to constantly talk to them; just spending time with them and observing them will be enough.

They need your focused attention –

 Not just quality time, but spending focused time with your kid is also very important. It is fine if you are focusing on your child for only 10 minutes a day, but make sure that you are at least trying to give your kid that "special time" every single day.

This will help you understand your child better and build a special bond with them. You can also try and arrange a few activities that you will exclusively do with him/her. Try to give them your undivided attention.

For example, you might spend time with your kid while driving them to school or while cooking, but that is not your undivided attention. Try to make time when all your attention will be on your child only.

Be aware of your child's environment –

 Research shows that the environment that your child is growing up in plays a huge role in their overall development. If a child grows up seeing his parents fighting, he is bound to develop toxic qualities, whereas if you provide a kid with a positive, warm and respectful environment, they will surely grow up to be better human beings.

The way you interact with your children, speak with them, and the things they see around them make a big difference in their psychological development.

Basic knowledge about your child's brain development is necessary –

 Some experts believe that the parents work as "neuroarchitects," meaning that parents play a great role in determining how a kid develops. When you interact with your child, it helps their brain cells develop.

A child's brain is shaped according to their experiences, which helps them react to various situations.

For example, if you influence your child's brain positively, they are bound to react to situations in a positive way. Whereas, if you hit your child or if the child grows up seeing violence, then they will respond violently to others.

Talk to your child –

Promoting a conversation with your child is very important. Most often, children do not speak if not spoken to, and as a parent, it is your duty to interact with them and promote conversations.

Encourage your child to talk and while they speak, listen to them carefully. Kids cannot express themselves properly, so while talking to them, make sure that you are listening to everything that they are saying carefully; that will help you understand their non-verbal cues.

Your Child's Early Brain Development Matters

You must know that as a child, Einstein was not very remarkable. He had difficulty in speaking and was taken to the doctor several times by his parents to see if he was alright. But what happened in his life that actually made him Einstein? Well, when he was young, he fell severely ill, and his father bought him a compass, and later his mother bought him a piano. Both things equally changed his brain.

Experts believe that children's brains develop during 2 to 7 years of age. During this time, the maximum development in the brain cells occurs. That is exactly why the experiences a child has during these phases last a lifetime. It is also during this time that every child has a wholistic educational development as well.

Here is how you can promote proper brain development in your child –

Don't scare them, rather encourage them to love the process of learning –

You must never let your kid get scared about learning. Your kid will only be able to learn and retain things if they start enjoying the process. The thought of learning new activities must bring joy to a kid and not be a reason for them to feel scared.

It does not matter if they are making mistakes; remember, mistakes are a part of learning. Remember, development is a process, and it takes daily effort. Also, stop labeling your kids and telling them things like "you are so smart" or "how can you be so dumb." Focus on persistence and praise the child for their enthusiasm.

Focus on quantity and not quality –

This is the time when you should not focus on the depth of the skills that the kids are developing; instead, during this time, you must focus on how many skills they are developing.

Engage your kid in a variety of activities – be it music, dance, sports, Math, poetry, etc. this will act as a foundation for their further development. Kids from 2 to 7 years old are ready to soak any skills introduced to them. Once their brain develops, they will get a lot of time to specialize later on in the future.

Focus on emotional intelligence as well –

Sure, you want your kid to be great at math and other academic and extra-curricular activities. But along with it, also remember to focus on their emotional intelligence.

Make sure your kids are also learning critical interpersonal skills like kindness, teamwork, and empathy. For example, ask your kid to help you with house chores. Even that will make them become a more considerate and empathetic person.

Tips to Respond to Your Kids so That They Listen

The way we talk to our kids has a lot of influence on them as a person. The kind of people around the kid determines what kind of personality they will develop. And as parents, you will face a lot of problems; one among them must certainly be your kid not communicating and responding to you properly.

Well, children do respond in various ways, some by shouting, some by crying, some by yelling, and others by feeling fearful. But your kid is responding the way you are treating him. So if you want your kids to listen to you, you will have to talk to them in a certain way. Here are a few tips that will help you communicate with your child better –

Call your child by their name –

Just like you love your name, even kids love their name. Kids are also very fickle-minded, so if you want to gain their attention and make them listen to you, call them by their name and when you have their attention, tell them whatever you have to.

Remember, there is no point in saying anything to your kid if they are not attentive. For example, tell them, "George, please do your homework," or "Emma, please eat your food."

Always use positive language –

 If you need to tell your kids sentences using "no" or "don't," they are more likely to do that particular thing. For example, if you keep telling your kid, "don't run with glass in your hand," "do not get dirty," and "no running inside the house," then you will find them doing the same thing. Rather than using such sentences and telling them what they must not do, tell them what they should do.

For example, "hold the glass properly". This type of change in your language will bring a major difference to your kid. Other than that, use positive behavior and respect the kid to get that in return.

For example, tell them, "thank you for helping me clean up the house," "you have worked so hard helping your sister; you must be tired." Such positivity will give your kid more confidence.

Make a connection with your child –

While interacting with your kid, make eye contact with them. Make sure you're getting down to their level and sitting with them while talking to them. Such habits will help them learn manners and help them learn to respect others as well. If you want respect from them, make sure you give them that yourself.

Use appropriate volume –

 You must have seen teachers at your school who keep on yelling at the top of their voice to make students listen to them, but do they become successful?

Well, no. Kids will not listen to you if you yell at them to prove your point. You must only talk to your kid when they have calmed down. If you keep on yelling at them during the appropriate time, even if you shout at them, they will end up ignoring you.

Other than that, you should also suggest them options and let them decide, stay away from nagging them, be a model to them, be a combination of gentle yet firm, and also initiate one-on-one conversation. It is true that having a kid can sometimes be difficult, but with the correct approach, you will surely be able to become a great parent. So if you want to know more about parenting, keep reading this book.

Exercise

Observe your child and write how they behave in various situations. This exercise will help you better connect and understand your child.

____

____

____

____

____

____

____

____

____

____

____

Chapter 2: Understanding Emotions

Emotions are the roots that keep a family together. They make a person who they truly are at an individual level, and at the same time, they form the base upon which the superstructure of a family stands. As new parents, I am sure you both have to deal with many new things.

It is true that with a baby comes a lot of responsibilities, but they also bring joys unheard of and immeasurable happiness. I am sure you are already experiencing the pure joys your baby brings to your life. There are few things as satisfying as seeing your child grow up to be a healthy and happy individual. As parents, what more can anyone ask for!

Having said that, I am sure you also realize that a lot of it is in your hands. Your baby right now is like a sponge. They will absorb everything that you expose them to. They will grow up learning everything that you teach them now.Needless to say, it is a huge responsibility where you, as parents, as your child's first and most important representative of the outside world, need to show them how they will conduct themselves.

That is where the need to experience and express the correct emotions comes into play. As an adult, I am sure you feel this every day, that the better we are at handling our emotions, the better we become in dealing with everything that happens to us.

Your child needs to get this correct teaching from the very beginning so that they can grow up to be more responsible, more open-minded, and of course, happier. I can understand if you feel apprehended or inhibited regarding your child's future. But don't you worry because I have got your back. Countless parents have felt the worries you are experiencing right now.

That is the reason, in this chapter, I have compiled for you some tips that will surely help you to understand your own and your child's emotions better.

Without further delay, let us get into some tested and proven ways that will give you far better control of the entire situation.

Encourage, Never Force

I once had a teacher back in school whose idea of making a child perform a job was to scare them or, better, hit them in case the child was not behaving. Do you know what the result of that "disciplinary action" was?

None of the students liked or respected her, and what more, no one could ever score well in the subject she used to teach simply because they were afraid of her. I am sure this is not what you have in mind for your child. Your child is growing up, taking the world as it is coming to them.

Everything is new, so there will be many things about which they feel a lot different than you do. And that is completely fine.

In case you feel that there is something that your child is doing wrong or could have done better, sit them down and have a conversation with them.

It is only natural for them to not like math and ignore the homework. Why so? Because as a child, they are not aware of the consequences. Tell them frankly how poor grades in school might hamper their future. But if you try to "force" your child to do something when they are unaware of what "not doing" it will lead to, you are simply giving them more reasons to repeat their behavior.

The push and pull of you forcing them and them becoming defiant will only hurt your child. The best way to make your child do or learn anything is to encourage them towards it. Don't misunderstand the term "encouragement" with "bribing here." They are not the same.

Don't make your child fall into the silly habit of doing something because you have promised them something in return. Instead, tell them what good they can do to themselves if they do it.

For example, before their exams, instead of saying they will get their favorite toy car if they score an "A," sit with them during their exam preps, make learning a fun process, and tell them that a good result will make you and their teacher feel proud of them, only because they have worked so hard. When your child feels that they are choosing the right thing and it is adding up to their loved ones feeling proud, they will not do it by force, but willingly.

Ways to put this in practice –

- Never compare them with others. Let them know that they are unique and you truly value them for who they are.

- Celebrate their accomplishments. Parties should not be restricted to birthdays or for coming first in class. It should also be for helping a friend or rescuing a puppy.

- Take an interest in their hobbies. They need to feel and understand that "productivity" is not restricted to societal standards of "accomplishments" but everything worthwhile and positive.

- Help them set goals. When they have something to look forward to, they will take the initiative and look forward to doing new things. That way, they will not feel any pressure.

Maintain Your Calm

Let me begin by telling you that I completely understand how difficult it is to always maintain your calm around your kid. As life is new for that little child, so is parenthood for you and your partner. You have your work to finish, a house to run, responsibilities to handle, and also a child to raise. It can be a lot. That is why you both need to stick together as partners and give it all you have.

No matter how justified your anger is, it can deeply impact your child. It is not only about things that are directly related to your kid. Even when your child sees that you both are fighting about something, they are going to be hurt.

Raising a kid is the toughest thing anyone has to do because, through that kid, you are rearing up a future citizen, individual whose physical, emotional, and psychological formations are dependent on you.

So you simply cannot take it lightly. Make sure you never fight amongst yourselves in front of your kid. As a child, it is from our parents that we learn things like forgiveness, kindness, and generosity. A child can never grow up to be kind or understanding when they see their parents being rude to each other.

Let your spouse deal with it when it comes to something your child has done that has angered you. Let your anger cool down, and then proceed further. Say your child has broken a beautiful vase while playing. Your instinct is to go and scold them and probably ground them for two days so that they will realize what wrong they have done. Let me make it clear to you that they will not understand. How can they understand when you have not made clear what exactly they have done wrong or what the consequences can be?

Instead, if you make them understand that that vase was a gift from grandma, and now she will be hurt, then your child will feel sorry. Next time, they will not play around with delicate objects and will listen to you when you give them instructions. Why?

Because they love grandma and they don't want to hurt her. Nothing can be achieved in anger. Any decision you make when you are really angry will only add up to you hurting your child and yourself emotionally.

Tips for maintaining your calm –

- Focus on the bigger picture. Ten years down the line, you won't be bothered whether your child finished their coloring book on time but whether they are happy and healthy.

- Take a time out. Instead of mindlessly allowing your frustration to create a scene, excuse yourself for some time and cool down. Things always look better when you are calm.

- Allow their mistakes. It is one thing to want what is good for your child and completely another to dictate everything they do.

- Consider the negative consequences. The moment you think about how it can hurt everyone involved, you will surely not let your anger rule you.

Disarm Your Triggers

We all have certain triggers that bring us to the edge. As is the nature of triggers, they threaten us at every point to make us lose control and topple down that edge. The moment you let your triggers get the better of you, you let yourself do things that you otherwise wouldn't have.

Now imagine you losing control in front of your child. That innocent kid probably has no idea what triggers mean in the first place. Your triggers could go off either because of something that your child has done unknowingly or also due to something that has happened to you otherwise.

You know better than anyone else what you can or cannot do or how you react when your triggers go off. Think for a second about whether that is appropriate to be shown in front of your child.

As a parent, you are their most potent parameter with which they measure the outside world. Anything you do automatically adds to them thinking the rest of the world to be that same way. I completely understand that it is not in our hands to anticipate when our triggers might go off, and that is the very reason you, as an individual and as a parent, need to work on it every day.

You have to disarm your triggers so that you do not expose your child to the harshness of life so early. They need to grow up to truly understand what these things mean for them to be empathetic towards you, respect your boundaries, and also deal with changes.

You need to understand that what is "little" or "less" to us is not so for a child. You might bring yourself under control very soon, but the damage might be done by then. Your kid might not show any external signs of it, but they will be impacted deep down. Life with a small child is unpredictable, to say the least. The amount of joy they bring to the household is unparalleled.

Simultaneously, they can surprise you often as well. As you steadily work on disarming your triggers, it will make you better equipped as parents to handle every situation without having to worry about losing control.

Ways to disarm your triggers –

- Identify what your triggers are.

- Keep a record of everything you go through when your triggers are set off.

- Make sure you and your spouse are well prepared at all times to handle the situation in case you get triggered.

- Take conscious steps every day to see to it that you remain in better control of yourself.

- Ask yourself what is more important. At any point, if you feel the triggers going off, talk to yourself. Ask yourself why you need to be in control. When it is about the well-being of your kid, things will be easier to take control of.

Teach Your Kids Boundaries

One of the biggest responsibilities that you have as a parent is to teach your child the concept of boundaries – boundaries in all aspects of life. In their home, in their school, for people whom they consider as family and whom they don't.

Your child will only learn to respect others when they see you doing that and also when you tell them why. Tell them that respecting boundaries does not only mean listening to others but also means keeping in check their behavior. Learning to control their anger becomes a primary factor then.

As a child, it is only natural for them to get angry when they do not get what they want. So far, they have never got the time or the chance to understand that the world does not revolve around them. As parents, I am sure you try your best to provide for your child in all ways possible.

So, when the time comes for them to face rejection, no matter how big or small that is, they get defensive. Try and understand that their anger or mood swings come less from being arrogant and more from being scared. Henceforth, they feel that they will not get those things simply because they haven't experienced something like that before. Rejection is foreign to them, and that makes them insecure. So what you do is just tell them honestly what the actual issue is, which will pacify them.

Something as simple as them asking for an ice cream, and you refusing them might make them cry and they might create a scene on the road. Instead of scolding them harshly, take them aside and tell them that you denying them ice cream does not mean they will never get one. It simply means that it is not the correct time to have one, and they can have one tomorrow or the day after. Or for example, if you see that your kid has taken a toy from their classmate without permission, make them understand that they can admire something from far but taking it crosses the boundary.

Instead of "if you do this again, I will throw away all your toys," ask them, "how will you feel if Tom takes your favorite toy without telling you?" Put the things in their perspective for them to give respect to what others will feel. You need to stop being angry at your child if you want them to learn anything. I used to hate math as a kid, but I still used to try only because my math teacher used to love me and encourage me to do better. Kids learn faster when they are not scared.

What you can do –

- Practice setting boundaries. Before you touch them, ask their permission. And when they come to you, tell them to take permission as well.

- Teach them the importance of "no." They need to know that they should firmly say a "no" if others force them to do things, they are uncomfortable with. Boundaries work both ways.

- Make a list of things that are improper for them to do and tell them why. You will be surprised how sensible children can be when they understand the matter.

- Always give examples, and that does not mean you will compare them with others. Giving live examples help them to put it into perspective.

Teach Your Kids Emotional Skills

Did you know that kids experience emotions just as adults do? It will probably be less in intensity but never less in manner. What's more, they find it harder to locate themselves among everything they are feeling simply because they have no prior experience of that.

As a parent, your role then is to help your kids express their emotions correctly and healthily. You need to take an active part and teach your child emotional skills, which will help them better grasp the entire situation. There are many ways for you to do it. No one knows your child better than you do. Take advantage of that fact and tune in to cues. Carefully observe your child's body language and see whether they are showing any signs of discomfort or hurt. A lot of times, children do not express themselves simply because they do not know how to.

It is a huge help if you can read their body language. It is for you to understand that no behavior is random. Children do not know how to fake situations or emotions. They are bound to express what they are feeling some way or the other. Whether they are happy or scared, or something else, can be understood even when they do not say it.

Teach your kid that it is not only healthy but also essential to not avoid what they are feeling and convey it to others. When they learn to recognize and eventually respect their own emotions, they will naturally extend that to others.

For example, teach them the difference between "good touch" and "bad touch." Make it clear to them that as parents, you are always ready to listen to them no matter how big or small their feelings might be. When they feel confident that they have the freedom to come and express their emotions to you, they will not take drastic or unhealthy steps or jump to wrong conclusions but deal with it maturely.

Some other ways in which you can help your child develop emotional skills are –

- Teach them to name each feeling so that they can validate all of them.

- Make them understand that what they are feeling, others do too. That way, they will learn to respect what others are going through.

- Be their role model. Unless you show your vulnerability to them, they won't learn to do the same. Show them the right way to deal with emotions.

- Make them understand that their emotions are valid and are respected by you. Show appreciation and praise when they do tell you.

- Listen to them. A lot of times, children might express non-verbally. Do not invalidate anything just because they are kids. When they are telling you something, listen carefully.

Parenthood is indeed a huge responsibility, but at the same time, it is that threshold in your life that adds a sense of completion to your being. I am sure that by now, you will be able to understand how to deal with all the emotional needs of your child.

As parents and as individuals, I am also certain that you both are aware of how to conduct yourself in front of your kid. The joy of seeing your child grow up well and being an active agent in making sure your child is fully attended to psychologically and emotionally is something you will give all your attention to. I hope you learn a lot in the process, but most importantly, I hope you evolve as a parent and lead a beautiful life with your child! All my best wishes!

Exercise

Identify what your triggers are. Keep a record of everything you go through when your triggers are set off.

Make sure you and your spouse are prepared to handle the situation in case you get triggered. Take conscious steps every day to see that you remain in better control of yourself. Ask yourself what is more important. Talk to yourself at any point if you feel the triggers going off. Ask yourself why you need to be in control. When it is about your kid's well-being, things will be easier to take control of.

Please list things that are improper for your kids to do and tell them why. You will be surprised how sensible children can be when they understand the matter.

Chapter 3: Making Connections With Your Child

As a parent, you will have to communicate with your child all the time since it is the primary way of teaching them what they have to do, how they have to behave, and also to know what they want. These interactions between a parent and child are often responsible for promoting a sense of responsibility in the child and building self-esteem.

How you communicate with your child will determine the kind of relationship you share with them. Healthy communication can foster an atmosphere of love, hope, acceptance, and support, which is essential for your child's growth.

Being a new parent, you may find it difficult to use words and actions effectively to communicate with your child. But we are here to take off the load for you by providing you with ways that would make both communicating with your child and parenting unchallenging.

Why Is Listening and Talking to Your Child an Important Part of Parenting?

After a long day of work, when you come back home, your child usually has a lot to say to you. Do you feel tempted to brush off their problems because you are tired, busy, or not in the mood?

Your child, on the other hand, expects to be heard. Both listening and communicating are crucial to good parenting and the development of the child. They are likely to share their concerns and problems as they grow older if you give them that space from early childhood. In order to show your child that you are actively listening, you will have to –

- Give complete attention to them.

- Focus on them at that moment. Put away everything else you are doing.

- Maintain eye contact with your child and get down to their level.

- To assure them that they have been heard and understood, either repeat what they said or reflect on their words.

Let us try to understand what you can do to actively listen to your child through an example – For instance, your child needs to leave for school at 8 in the morning, and you have a few minutes to make your family breakfast. In the meanwhile, your child comes out crying and complaining that they have been hit by their brother and have had their toy snatched away.

Since you do not have much time, you feel tempted to just keep nodding while making breakfast. But you decide to show your child that you are paying attention to them and actively listening to what they have been saying. You stop your work, face them, make eye contact, and summarize what they had been saying all this while. You ask them how they may be feeling. Doing so would make them feel that all your attention at the moment is towards them and that their emotions matter to you. Reflection is important as it shows your active participation in understanding your child and leaves more chances of improving communication with them as when you reflect, you give attention to their words, making them want to talk more.

How to Improve Your Communication Skills With Your Child?

Communication is the key to healthy parenting. It is perhaps the most rewarding and pleasurable part of parenting. Through daily interactions, your child will absorb information and learn the ways of the world. The more you communicate and interact with them, the more they learn. Here are some ways you can improve your communication with your child –

Give wait time –

Many of us have the habit of chiming in with what we have to say before we let the other person finish the sentence. You cannot do this with your child. Wait for at least five to ten seconds after they have finished speaking, or give them that much time to organize their thoughts.

For instance, sometimes, your child may not be able to communicate their feelings because they may be crying incessantly. In such a situation, wait for them to finish up, gather thoughts, and tell you how they may be feeling.

Do not correct your child all the time –

If you have the habit of over-correcting your child, please stop! If your intention is to improve your communication with your child, over-correcting them will take you the opposite way.

The more you demand they say something correctly, the more it may get worse. Overcorrecting may discourage them from talking at all; you make it sound like a negative thing to them.

Treat your child like a communication partner –

This could be a bit tricky since you have to communicate with them how you would talk to an adult, and at the same time, keep in mind that they are children.

Talking to them like adults does not mean using big words or complicated expressions. Say you do not understand what they may be saying. Instead of baby talking them, try to guess what they could be saying.

Switch off the television –

It's easier for parents to keep their children engaged by putting on the television and giving them a break, but I will advise you to keep it off as much as possible. This will help your child learn to entertain themselves and also develop better communication skills.

Read to them –

Apart from just reading them stories, you can read the signs on the street or the instructions that come behind the box of their toys. Even when you read them stories, you do not need to read every word or line. You can show them pictures and talk about them.

Say you are reading the story of Snow White. Show them the pictures of the seven dwarfs and say how they seem to be helping the poor girl.

With this, you get to accomplish two things –

o   Help your child to use their imagination.

o   Strengthen the receptive and expressive skills of your child.

Ask open-ended questions –

Such questions are not the typical 'yes' or 'no' questions. They give your child the scope to think and express. For example, instead of asking them if they liked a book or not, ask them which part of the book they liked.

However, be careful not to bombard them with too many questions. You must come across to them as a model conversation partner and not as a tester. Too many questions do not ensure enhanced language skills.

Repeat words –

Try to repeat words as many times as you can, as children need to hear a word at least a hundred times before they learn to utter it. Sing songs from their favorite cartoon. Remember, repetition is the key to learning and an excellent way of improving their communication skills.

Explain consequences –

You do not need to ground your child for being naughty. You can instead explain the situation and the consequences of their actions. This definitely require some patience and practice; however, it will help them develop stronger reasoning skills in the long run. For instance, your child is standing on a chair and refusing to come down. Explain that it is going to hurt if they fall down.

Praise your child for talking –

This again requires some balance. Every time your child says something, you do not need to shower them with praises. For instance, if your child pronounces a name correctly or uses the vocabulary you have been teaching them, you can compliment them for learning well. Or when they talk comprehensively, you can praise them for it.

How to Become More Patient as a Parent?

Parenting is a tough job, and as first-time parents, you are likely to lose your calm. Being a patient parent is important for improving your child's behavior, but it is not as easy as it sounds. Here are some tips that can help you to grow your patience –

Ask yourself 'why?' –

Would you believe if you were told that your child acts up not because they want to be a rebel? They may do so because they are tired or sick or need a little more care and attention.

Every time your child is not at their best behavior, it does not indicate they have a behavioral problem. Therefore, the next time they throw a tantrum, ask yourself why they may be doing so or try listening to your kid. Get down to their level and ask what is bothering them.

Try redirections –

Your child will need to be redirected every once in a while. They may be having a tantrum, or you need to pull them away from a loud toy.

Redirecting helps with such situations. You will simply have to divert their attention toward something else. You can ask them if they want to color, build something, or if they are hungry.

Set smaller goals –

You will not become patient overnight, so do not be too hard on yourself. Practice and repetition will get you there slowly. Do not try to change everything immediately. Instead, set smaller goals. Find out areas where you think you need more patience.

It could be dealing with your child's morning routine or teaching them to clean up their toys. Once you have identified the area, take small steps towards growing your patience. Once you feel a habit has been solidified, you can move on to the next one.

Don't overlook your own needs –

 Parents, while tending to their child's needs, may forget that they have needs too. Feed both your soul and mind. Hydrate yourself or eat something before dealing with your child's behavior.

Do something that can lighten up your mood if you are having a tough time so that you may come back to the problem in a more creative, constructive, and calm manner.

If you ever feel guilty looking after your own needs, think of it in a positive way. Tell yourself that you will have better energy to deal with your child if you take care of yourself.

Get a helping hand –

There is no shame if you call someone to give you a helping hand. Maybe hire a babysitter once or twice a week so that you can have some time to yourself. Childcare help is great for preschoolers as it slowly teaches them to be independent and develop social skills.

How to Build Positive Self-Esteem?

If your child feels good about themselves, they are more likely to want to try new things and try their best at it. Their ability to do something makes them feel proud and also helps them to cope with their mistakes. On the other hand, if your child has low self-esteem, they are likely to be unsure about themselves, and it may affect their overall growth and development.

As your child grows, their self-esteem can grow too. It starts to develop early in every child and develops slowly over time. The feeling of safety, security, love, and warmth can promote the growth of self-esteem in them. As a parent, here are some ways in which you can build positive self-esteem in your child.

Help them learn to do things –

Your child has something new to learn at every age. Things like your child taking their first step or even learning to hold a cup sparks a sense of delight. As they grow up, learning things like brushing their teeth and getting dressed by themselves can grow their self-esteem.

Demonstrate and help your child when teaching new things –

Your child will learn better if you show them how to do a task, for instance, brushing their hair. Then leave them to do it on their own even if they make mistakes. Give them the chance to learn, try, and feel proud.

Compliment your child –

When you praise your kids, it shows that you are proud of them. However, too much praise can backfire, which is why you should do it wisely. How?

o   Do not praise them unnecessarily or too much. Let them earn praise. For example, telling your child they played well even when they know they did not will feel fake. You can instead assure them that they will do better next time.

o   Praise their efforts instead of just praising the results. For instance, your child is working on a project. You can tell them that they are getting better at their work without waiting to see what grades they get for it.

Be a good role model –

When your child sees you putting effort every day while making a meal or doing chores, they also put effort while cleaning their toys or doing homework. Also, the right attitude counts too. Teach your child to do their tasks cheerfully by setting an example for them.

Do not criticize them harshly –

Children have the habit of translating the words they hear from others into how they feel about themselves. If they hear negative things about themselves, it may hurt their self-esteem. This is why when correcting them, you have to be patient and careful with the words you use.

Focus on their strengths –

Help your child to develop whatever they are good at. Focusing on their strengths will make them feel good about themselves.

Encourage your child to help and give –

When your child sees that what they do matters to others, their self-esteem grows automatically. They can help anybody, anywhere, be it helping to clean at home or helping a friend at school.

How Can You Teach Basic Social Skills to Your Child?

Humans are social beings, and the moment a child is born, the process of socialization begins. A child needs to learn social skills to be a part of society, interact with others, converse, make friends, be responsible for their behavior, and much more. Here are five ways in which you can teach social skills to your child –

Encourage them to make eye contact –

Encourage your child to maintain eye contact when talking to someone as it is essential for effective communication and building confidence. This, however, requires to be practiced every day. You can tell your child to talk to their toys or narrate stories while looking into your eyes.

Teach them emotions –

Allow your child to imitate different kinds of emotions like anger, happiness, disappointment, nervousness, tiredness, terror, danger, excitement, joyfulness, etc. For doing so, let them identify emotions from cards or pictures. It will help them to not only differentiate between emotions but also express themselves better.

To teach them, you must also make a habit of communicating what things make you feel what kind of emotions. So, when they make mischief next time, your straight face can communicate that you are upset.

Make them communicate –

 You must teach your child to interact, express, and respond to social stimuli both verbally and non-verbally. Teach them how they can greet or respond to someone. As a parent, talk to them every day and make it a habit to use words like 'please,' 'thank you,' etc., in your speech.

Give them the right environment –

A child who grows up alone will find it difficult to interact with others. As a parent, make sure that you give them company or the opportunity to interact with other people. For this, you can send them to playschool, hobby classes, or playgrounds where they can interact with other children.

Prepare them for higher social skills –

As your child grows up, try to up their social skills too. If they learn to communicate and express themselves, they are likely to be able to handle complex situations in life. Make sure that your child maintains good communication channels, learns to resolve conflict, can speak well in public, learn to negotiate, etc.

How Can You Teach Your Child to Listen?

You have very politely asked your child to do something, but they maintain radio silence as if they have not heard you at all. You slowly enter the cycle of repeating and reminding the same thing, and after a point, the fuse blows, and you begin screaming your demands. Here are some ways by which you can handle your child's unresponsiveness and teach them to listen –

Get on their level –

Here, remember that proximity is the key. You should not be shouting orders or talking down to them. Instead, look in their eyes so that you may have their attention and instruct them on what needs to be done.

Give clear instructions –

When you use words like 'don't' and 'no,' your child faces confusion. For instance, you tell your child not to touch something; they have to first stop what they are doing and think of an alternate behavior. Instead, practice giving clear instructions to your child like what they should 'do.'

Say 'yes' –

If you have the habit of saying no to every request your child makes, then they are likely to never take your permission seriously. Look for reasons where you can agree to them more often.

For instance, they want to go to the park but that day seems impossible for you. Instead of saying no, tell them that a visit to

the park sounds exciting and the weekend would be the perfect
time to visit – when they hear more yeses, the chances of your
child tuning in increases.

Shorten your speech –

Children will not be able to follow instructions that are long.
Therefore, keep your speech as short and concise as you can so
that they may not lose you midway.

Thank them in advance –

You thanking your child in advance can be a leap of faith, but it
can guide them to make an appropriate choice. For instance,
thank your child for keeping their room tidy even before they
have done it. Your child will be more likely to clean up if you
use this technique instead of when you warn them of the
consequences if they do not clean up.

Your bond with your child will depend on how you
communicate with them. As a parent, you may want to know
everything that is going on in their mind. Only with effective
communication will it be possible for you to deepen your
relationship with your child.

If you are enjoying this book or find it helpful. Please help us by writing a short review on Amazon. Your support makes a difference, and I read your reviews personally. So I can get your feedback and make this book even better.

To leave a review, you must go to amazon and type Parenting Toddlers by Trista frost. Click on the book; you will find the review option at the bottom of the page.

Thanks a lot for your support.

Chapter 4: Basics of parenting

I have dedicated this chapter to answering all your probing questions. Questions that can seem to overwhelm at times but whose answers are absolutely essential. Parenthood is nothing short of a rollercoaster ride. But why not make it a fun one instead of getting all panicky, right! It is, after all, in your hands to make of any given situation however you want that to be, given it is your child and your family.

Questions like "How can I make my child do chores willingly?" "What do I do when my child is not learning to talk fast enough?" or even "When is the best time to start schooling my kid?" are questions that parents have been facing.

Your parents have faced them, and so will your next generation. All your worries are justified, and they all have very plausible solutions. I understand that you feel overwhelmed at times and that it worries you, given that your child's future is in question. But I always believe that problems can be solved very easily provided you look at them differently.

When it comes to raising your child to be a responsible adult, do not let yourself be pestered with worries all the time. Instead, look at it as a medium of endless opportunities for both you and your kid. It is not only your kid who is getting to learn new things; it is also you and your partner who are learning so much. So instead of letting it seem like a difficult school project given by a strict teacher, think of it as a fun assignment that is going to let you discover new sides of your child and also of yourself. As I have already mentioned, I am going to answer some of the most prominent questions that parents ask while raising a kid. So, without further delay, let me get to it.

Letting Your Kid Take Responsibilities Around the House

A huge part of growing up to be a responsible human being comes from learning to take responsibility, and what better place than home to start doing it right? Instead of unnecessarily pampering your child, give them some light work that is to be done around the house, which will not seem like a burden to them. I am sure you were raised in a similar way.

When I was a kid, my mom had given me the responsibility of filling up the water bottles each morning. But instead of making it sound like an order, she had told me, "Because you fill the bottles each morning, all of us get to drink water and have to never worry about seeing our bottles empty." When you see it from an adult's perspective, it can sound silly, but to a child of ten years, this felt like a really special thing to do.

Believe it or not, I had never gotten out of that habit and had continued doing it till I had moved out of my parent's house. Because mom had put it in a way where I felt what I was doing was good and essential, it never felt like a burden to me. I am giving you a few very useful tips which will help you make your child take responsibility around the house.

Do Not Make It Seem Like a Burden —

 Like I was just telling you, I never felt like not doing what mom told me to do simply because she never made it sound like a compulsion. Your child will do all the chores you ask them to do when they feel it is not a compulsion.

Kids are really smart, and as parents, one of the best things to do is to give them the respect that they deserve. Sit them down and make them understand the necessity of the work that they need to do. Along with that, tell them that you trust them to do that work responsibly.

So instead of "If you do not clean your room, you will not go out to play," tell them, "Keep your room neat and clean because I know you do not want mommy to worry." Before they know it, doing that chore will become a habit.

When your kid does not feel pressured, they will do it naturally without complaining. Kids hate it when you treat them like kids. It is funny but true.

So, while giving them responsibilities, do not put it in a way that "You need to do it because kids have to learn," etc.; just tell them that adults do it too. That will make them feel like they are growing up and are being treated respectfully.

Show Them That Everyone Else is Doing Chores as Well —

The best way for kids to learn anything new is to see their elders doing those same things. Each and every value that you want to imbibe in your child will only happen when they see you practicing exactly what you are preaching.

That is why the easiest way your child will learn to take up responsibilities and do chores is when they see everyone else doing those as well.

When you are giving your child any responsibility, let them understand that everyone else in the family does their respective work as well. My mom used to always make it clear to my siblings and me that for a household to function properly, everyone needs to do their needful.

We always knew that mom and dad had their fixed chores to complete, which is why it came to doing our chores; it somehow made me and my siblings feel better connected with our family.

Be transparent with them and let them understand that their participation is essential and deeply respected as a family. Simple things like " divide the work and finish it fast so that we can sit and watch a movie together" will work far better than you ordering them around.

Ask for Their Inputs —

An ideal family should be a lot like a democracy, where each member is given their due importance, and everyone's views are taken into account. That includes your kids as well.

Yes, you heard me right. No matter how small they are or how trivial that work is, you should talk to them beforehand and ask what they think of it. That way, they will know that their opinion matters as well as everyone else's.

Of course, I am not talking about discussing tax bills or car insurance with your toddler. But when you are dividing the house chores, and allotting them their work, take their views into account as well. Give them options and let them choose.

Say, for example, ask them which one they prefer, filling up water bottles, dusting the pieces of furniture, or watering the plants. When they choose, they will be more comfortable with the work assigned.

At the same time, if they do not want to work on a certain day, allow them that once in a while. It is their house and not prison. They should feel that their comfort and discomfort are given priority.

Give Them Only What They Can Handle —

As parents, I am sure you knew this even before you started reading this, that, as elders, and especially as parents, you can make a child work only as much as they can actually take on their plate. Doing household chores and taking responsibility is a must for every person.

The faster a child is brought into the framework of how responsibilities work, the better it is for them.

But that being said, you simply cannot expect your child to do the work that adults are supposed to do. In the hope of teaching them something, do not push them to an extent where it becomes physically and mentally impossible for them to cope with it. It is better to start small.

There is no point in becoming one of those parents who takes pride in comparing their kids to others. Don't ever be like them. Instead, let your child grow up at a pace that they are comfortable with and which is healthy for them.

It can start with them arranging their toys, followed by cleaning their room. Dusting the pieces of furniture to mow the lawn.

Increase the intensity of the chores as they grow up. That way, they will learn to complete every work fully and also respect what they are doing.

Keep in mind that the objective is to give them responsibilities and make them understand why that is essential for them. You can employ these methods without a doubt, and I am sure they will bring positive results.

Teach Your Child to be Flexible and Cooperative

It is essential that your child learns about flexibility and cooperation from an early age. We live in a society surrounded by people of varied interests and lifestyle choices. Your kid will find it difficult to navigate their way unless they know how to bend a little instead of breaking. While they go to school, they will come in contact with different kids, all coming from different families.

It is only natural for everyone to be different. When your child is cooperative, it is a piece of cake to maintain a peaceful and friendly relationship with everyone around.

What's more, this will become a weapon and a blessing as they grow up. What better time to teach them to be flexible and cooperative than this, right? Let me give you a few tips for that.

Take Turns with Your Child –

"Kevin, you just played with your doll. It is your cousin's turn now." Or "Maya, I know you love that car, but Kevin loves it too. He should also get a chance to play with it, right?" this is what I am talking about.

Teaching your child something new does not have to be so serious or difficult at all. When you put those values in their perspective, it just becomes easier for them to understand what is to be done.

A very common mistake that few parents make is teaching their kids in a way in which kids do not understand. That is wrong and also burdensome for the kid. Your child is, after all, just a baby.

You cannot expect them to understand the intensity of values so soon, right? Imagine how all of us were when we were kids. That is the reason when you are trying to teach your child to be flexible and cooperative, just teach them in a way that they understand.

Give Them Choices, But Wisely –

It falls upon you to give them choices. The meaning of cooperation or being flexible rests upon their abilities to learn the importance of choices, both their own and that of others. When you give them choices, it fills them with a sense of power, and they start acting more responsibly. When you give them certain orders, you need to put them in a way that seems that they too want that.

That will teach them to be flexible. Say you have prepared two kinds of greens for dinner; when you know that having any one of them will do, ask them which one they want. Let them choose, and they will never waste it. But say it is their time to take a nap.

Do not ask, "Do you want to take a nap now?" Chances are they will say "no." Instead, put it like, "You and I are going to take a nap now, okay? We are tired after studying, so let us take a quick nap." When you make it sound like that, they are bound to listen. So make sure your choices are given wisely.

Give Them Their Due Recognition –

I truly believe that no matter what the age of a person is, you need to give them their due recognition. Credit should be given where it is due. It especially works like magic with kids.

You need to remember that you are your kid's first and most potent representatives of the outside world as parents. Every word you say, actions you take, and the emotion you showcase are all basically the guidelines for your child to form their mindset and create their viewpoints.

 So, when your child sees that they get praised by you after doing a certain work, it is only natural for them to make up their mind that what they are doing is right. They will continue doing so if not for anything else but to be praised by you. Use this opportunity to make them learn what is right and what is not; when they do anything well, praise them.

Let them know that their act is appreciated. It could be as simple as sharing a bar of chocolate with their friends or keeping their room tidy, or helping you around the house. Make sure they know that their acts of cooperation and flexibility are appreciated, and that way, they will continue doing so.

A simple thing like "Kevin, I am very proud that you cleaned your room so well" or "You did a great job by sharing your candy" can mean a lot to your child.

Explain Better –

Do not ever think that your child is not smart enough just because they are young. This is the age where like a sponge, they absorb everything that they see around them. You, as parents, are the direct examples from whom they learn everything.

So instead of beating around the bush, it is always best to put something as simple as possible. The more transparent you are, the faster your child will learn and understand. Somebody I know, who is a single father of two beautiful kids, always tells me that 'do not treat your kids in a way in which you will not like to be to be treated yourself.'

When explaining something, do not hide details, thinking they will not understand. Instead, put it in a way that builds trust, where they know they are not being robbed of any information.

Say, for example, you want them to cooperate with you and not come near the oven while you are cooking. Instead of telling "Mommy will be very mad if you come in the kitchen," which honestly does not make much sense, tell them, "This fire can harm you and me both. I am sure you do not want that, right? So come in the kitchen after I am done cooking, Okay?" It is simpler and easier to understand.

Let Helpfulness Pave the Way

Being kind and helpful is one of the greatest virtues that you can imbibe in your child. One of the best gifts that we as humans can give to others is to be kind to them and help them in times of need. Your child should learn from your ways in which they can be helpful to others so that this does not seem like an added burden but the most natural thing to do. Let's see a few ways in which you can easily teach them the importance and need for helpfulness.

Celebrate When They Are Spontaneously Helpful –

"Kevin, you did a great job today helping me in the kitchen. Let us go for ice cream!" Something like this will definitely create a substantial impact on their mind. Your child will understand that helpfulness is something that is appreciated and celebrated. Your celebrations might not always be through material goods.

It could also be watching their favorite movie together or playing with them their favorite game. The objective here is to make them realize that what they have done is a good thing and should be continued.

Their acts of spontaneous helpfulness might be done with or without them understanding what they are doing. When you celebrate with them, it just makes it special for them.

Practice What You Preach –

Your kid learns best from what they see is going on in the house. Every value that you speak of will start making more sense to them when they see you applying those in real life. When they see that you are doing exactly what you are asking them to do, it just makes it all the more natural for them to start practicing it.

Unless they see you doing it as well, it fails to become a natural habit but remains a forced command from the elders. I am sure you already help each other out in the family. Make sure your child takes notice of that.

You do not need to go out of the way to make it visible, but even simple things like "Kevin, did you see how daddy was helping me out in the garden today? Let us do it tomorrow and finish sowing the seeds, alright?" will show them how, what they are being asked to do, is something that everyone else does naturally as well.

Teach When They Should Not Be Helpful as Well –

Yes, you read that right. I am talking about teaching your child to choose truth over helping someone when the need comes. Being helpful is important, but your child needs to learn when they are being taken advantage of.

Say your daughter has completed her homework much before the due date. Now one of the friends has come asking her to finish her homework as well, given she hasn't done it. It is one thing to help a friend with homework, but in this case, finishing their homework will just mean being taken advantage of.

That is wrong, and your daughter needs to say a firm "no" to her friend. She might think that she is being helpful, but actually, she is just opening the path for more such situations to occur in the future.

Make Them Feel Secure –

Studies have shown that emotional and psychological security is directly connected with a child's growth and development of values.

The contrary happens when they feel scared or threatened. A child will not be ready to share their toys or food with others if they have been threatened to do it in any previous situation.

They might also be less enthusiastic about helping others in case they had been scared on any previous occasion regarding not doing the same. The other day, my niece came from school and told me that her teacher scolded her today for not sharing her pencil with her bench partner.

 I asked her why she didn't do it, and as expected, she replied, "I did not want to share my pencil because my teacher had scolded me yesterday as well." When your child feels safe and secure to do a certain thing, only then will they understand its value.

Motivate Your Child

Kids are supremely intelligent and also witty. You should never take them for granted. My mom is a teacher, and I have always heard from her that the best way one can teach a child is to motivate them to do something. We, as adults, need to understand that no matter how small a child is, they are, after all, separate individuals.

We cannot "make" them do something just because we want to or because we have more power. They need to be actually wanting to do that thing. So, the best we can do is to inspire them and motivate them so that they willingly do it. Here are some tips for you to try.

Don't Try to Motivate the Traditional Way –

Gone are the days when the traditional ways of motivating your child used to work. "over-praising," "conditional-praising," "nagging," "forcing," "threatening," etc., are all ways that parents used to employ to "motivate" their kids in the past. Do not commit that mistake because it will have a very bad impact on your child. Over-praising them for something simple will twist their mind.

Conditional praising is almost like bribing where you don't actually care about them, but in order to get a job done, you simply use them emotionally. Nagging, forcing, or threatening are just examples of parents having a twisted mentality to make their children do things that they could not do themselves.

It honestly does not make any sense and should be stopped as soon as possible. Motivating your child has got nothing to do with making them do things that they actually do not want to do.

Don't Try to Control Them, But Let Them Enjoy the Task –

 Get this straight- a controlling parent can NEVER motivate a child. Unless your child actually enjoys what you are asking them to do, it will only be a command from you that they are trying to obey because they are scared of you. I am sure, as parents, your main aim is to see your child physically and emotionally healthy right?

So why at all put them through an emotional crisis? I am sure that when you tell your child to do something, you have their best in mind. But at the end of the day, your child needs to enjoy that task.

As parents, I will suggest you create a healthy learning environment in the house, where your child does not fear to try out new things, for they know you are there to support them.

When you let your children have the freedom to try out new things, they will never be afraid of anything. Instead of "You have to do it if you want to get good grades," tell them, "It is okay if you want to try out something new. Just make sure to have fun while learning something new."

Tell Them Why Something is Important –

There could be times when your child fails to realize the importance of something and does not do it. It is absolutely natural, given that, after all, they are just kids. It is during these times that you, as parents, should sit them down and tell them frankly why it is important for them.

By this, in no way do I mean you need to force them or pressurize them. But talk to them through the entire process and use easy examples so that they can understand why it will be good for them.

You will notice that many a time, even when a child does not show interest in something initially, they can change their mind and get motivated when they start doing it.

Do not start scolding your kid because they are not doing something you had asked them to do. Kids tend not to do things which they find unnecessary. It is not because they are disrespectful or arrogant.

So it is better to just tell them why it is important so that you can develop motivation in them. The moment they realize it is something good, they will start taking an interest in the work.

Understand That it is Their Decision-

You have to help them decide what they want, and most importantly, you have to let them decide. I understand that you fear that they might fail. But let me assure you that it is absolutely alright. Do you remember the first time your child learned how to cycle?

They had fallen down, right? It is only natural for any one of us to fail at times before we learn to do something. But that does not mean they are not going to get better.

Your child needs to be able to decide on their own, of course with your guidance and support, for them to actually learn something. Make sure that your child always has that assurance from you that they know they are not alone. That itself is the biggest motivation you can give them.

When and How to Reward Your Child

It is crucial that your child knows that you are proud of them and that the efforts they take in everyday life are noticed and appreciated by you. You see, child psychology is very complex. One would think that because they are so small, they do not understand a lot of things. That is where parents go wrong. Children are extremely intuitive, and they understand when they are appreciated and when they are not.

Rewarding your child is essential to help them build a healthy psyche. When I talk about rewarding, I do not only restrict that to tangible gifts.

Yes, tangible gifts are indeed important at times. But it is not a good idea to make a little child get habituated to that. Intangible rewards are equally important and, at times, more so. Here, I am listing a few tips for you to take note of, through which you will get an idea regarding how to and when to reward your child.

Do Not Confuse Rewarding with Bribing –

As much as it is for your kids to understand, as parents, you need to understand as well that rewards are not bribes. Do not help your kid develop the mentality where they become ready to do something only when there is a reward waiting.

In case they get hold of this habit, it will be extremely difficult to make them do anything substantial. The bribe will become more important than the work itself, and we most definitely do not want that.

Another suggestion, it is best not to involve money in the equation. You can reward your child in various ways, but using money to get them to do something might not be a good idea. You can obviously gift them some extra money to spend occasionally, but the money itself should never become the main incentive.

Children might misunderstand the intent and say yes to anything elders ask them to do when they see they are earning in return. So let them understand the difference between "If you do your homework on time, I will give you ten bucks" and "I am very happy with your conduct today. You deserve ice cream for that."

Reward Their Progress and Don't Force for Perfection-

You rewarding them will depend on what your parameters are for doing a good deed. That is why you, as parents, should realize what it is that you want for your kid. Is it perfection, or is it progress? Let me be frank with you. Perfection is a myth. So do not be under that illusion that your kid will be perfect in something, and only then will you reward them.

If it is so, then your kid will never be rewarded, and no matter what efforts they put in, you will never be satisfied.

As parents, what you should look for instead, is progress. At the end of the day, it is progress that matters, isn't it? Don't you think that you want to see your child, happy and healthy, voluntarily progressing towards their goals?

That is the reason when you see their progress or even their honest efforts, make sure you reward them. It should not be "You will get your favorite toy if you score a 100 on your math test" but "I know that you have put in a lot of effort in your exams. Your marks have increased a lot, and that deserves a celebration."

Focus on Intangible Rewards –

Just as I have mentioned before, rewarding with intangible goods are as important as rewarding with tangible ones. What exactly do I mean by that? Well, you see, human beings, especially kids, are thirsty for love and affection. When they see that through your actions towards them, they are equally happy as when you gift them a material object.

Say, for example, your kid has helped an injured puppy on the road. This act of kindness deserves a reward, right? That reward will teach them to do this good deed again. So, instead of buying them something, let them choose the menu for the family dinner or let them choose the movie to be watched for that weekend. Hug them and let them know how proud you are of that action.

This will make them feel special as well as empowered. Intangible rewards might include you allowing them to stay up a little late that night, playing a bit more, or baking together with their favorite cookies. It can be any act of goodness that involves them being happy and made to feel special. As long as your kid feels their act is being appreciated, they will value it.

Times You Should Ignore Your Child's Behavior

Children do not know how to frame facts or lie as adults do. But having said that, I am sure you are aware that children, at times, do things solely to get their parent's attention or when they are seeking validation. These are the times you need to avoid them.

When you see that there is nothing physically wrong, and there has been no reason for them to be emotionally hurt as well, the chances are that they are doing it to grab your attention.

It is best to ignore them and not support such behavior. In most cases, they will stop after the first few attempts, given they know it is not helping their cause. Let us look at some of the ways when you need to ignore your child.

Don't Confuse Destructive Behavior with Misbehavior

Before I get into details of how and why you should ignore your child, it is essential for you to understand the difference between your child misbehaving and your child showing destructive behaviors.

It is not the same when your child throws a tantrum regarding not going to school and them harming themselves because they are upset over something.

Both are different, and the latter can have dangerous results if you ignore that. It is normal for a child to misbehave simply because they are ignorant of the proper way of civilized conduct.

But it is absolutely not normal for a child to harm themselves unless something is seriously wrong. If they are showing signs of destructive behavior, you must get to the root of it and know what is troubling them. Take them to a child psychologist if needed. Whatever it is, do not ignore that. As parents, you need to be able to differentiate what is what.

Ignoring Does Not Mean Rebuking –

Now, coming to the ignoring part, do not confuse ignoring with rebuking. Remember that when your child is throwing a tantrum, their aim is to get your attention in whichever way possible. It could be by you getting them what they want or, at times, you simply leaving what you were doing and coming to them. Even if you come to rebuke them, they will have fulfilled their purpose. That is not what you want when you want to rectify their tantrum.

Let's say they are crying in the middle of the road for ice cream. It is only natural for you to scold them and bring them home or, worse, buy that ice cream so that they stop creating a scene.

But the best way for them to stop whining is to pretend you cannot see or hear what they are saying.

Take their hand and go about your way. Let them cry or whine. Do not worry about others on the road because, in all probability, they too have faced a similar situation with their kids. When your child sees that no amount of crying is having any effect on you, they will get tired and stop after a point. Mission accomplished!

Pair Ignoring with Giving Attention –

Always keep your ultimate objective in mind. Why are you ignoring certain behaviors of your child? It is to make them understand that certain behaviors are not appreciated, and all demands cannot be kept. But that is not all. Keep in mind that it is a child we are dealing with here. Things are either black or white for them.

Their brains are not yet accustomed to understanding things in between.

So, when you are not entertaining a certain kind of behavior because it is undesirable, they need to be shown clearly what the behavior is that will be accepted as well. Only then will they understand what is good and what is bad. So what you need to do is pair your attitude of ignoring and giving them attention based on how they are behaving.

Say they threw a tantrum and you ignored it effectively; your child might not understand what is going on. But when you give them their deserved attention after something good they have done, their understanding will slowly start falling in place. When this is repeated, things will eventually become clear to them. Let's take the previous example; just as you had ignored them during that ice cream fiasco, you give them attention after they have come home and cleaned up their room.

Communicate Why You Are Ignoring Them –

It might be that your child is misbehaving at a certain moment, but they are doing it, as I mentioned, to seek validation. They are kids, and they, at that point, do not know any better. But that does not mean they do not deserve to know why they are being ignored.

The chances are that the first time you ignore them, they will not even understand what happened. As you start ignoring their tantrums more and more, they will start getting confused, they will feel hurt, and a phase will also come where they will throw more tantrums simply because you are not giving them attention.

Instead of letting this situation get worsen, the best way to deal with it is to tell them honestly why you are ignoring them. I suggest you sit with them after the episode is over and they have calmed down and tell them what happened exactly. "Kevin, the fact that you were screaming on the road was irritating, unreasonable, and embarrassing for me. So I ignored you. do not repeat it if you don't want me to ignore you again." The better you communicate with them, the faster they will understand their mistake.

Walk the Steps with Your Child

I know that you have been eagerly waiting for your child's first steps. In general, a child starts walking at the age of 12 months. But honestly, that is not the ultimate indicator of measurement. Many children learn to walk before or well after this age bar, and unless it is really late, you really don't need to worry about it.

Some parents fear that in case their child starts walking late, it is an indication of them not being as smart as they are supposed to be. But it is not true. No scientific evidence shows any truth in that assumption. In case it has been almost 20 months and your child is still not walking, you should consult your pediatrician. But before that, it's time for you to relax. Let your baby become more comfortable and confident with the whole process, and then take those adorable steps forward.

Few signs that you should look out for which indicate that it is time for you to take those first steps are –

- Look whether they are becoming more adventurous. It is a sign that they are gaining confidence. Increasing their crawling speed only means that it is not enough for them anymore. They will soon want to walk.

- See whether your child can walk with your assistance. If yes, know for a fact they are going to try it on their own soon.

- A change in their regular sleep pattern is also an indication. Walking is a big physical development for a child. This comes with other physical changes as well, leaving a baby slightly less tolerant and irritated at times. Don't worry; it's absolutely normal.

I understand your worry when your baby is taking the time to walk. So what can you do in such a situation –

- Look how the other motor skills are developing in your child. If they are able to crawl, stand up with support from furniture, bounce, etc., then there is nothing to worry about. Your baby will catch up soon and start walking.

- If your baby was born prematurely, it might take a bit more time than others to walk. So do not worry and have patience.

- Help your baby to walk. As they are near the walking age, instead of carrying them, urge them to walk. Create a safe environment in the house for them to explore.

Opening the Gates of Words

I am sure you have spent days waiting to hear that first word from your baby's lips. Nothing is sweeter to parents than that. Some might start talking early, and others might take some time. Just like walking, when they start to talk is not a sign of intelligence. Of course, it is a sign of giftedness for children who start talking early, but that is not similar to "understanding."

So do not worry if your child is taking time, because that does not mean they are any less intelligent. In case you want to ease the process of talking to your kid, you can try some ways to urge them towards it.

- Talk to them all the time. During their meals, when you are bathing them or clothing them, make sure you talk to them constantly. Let them get more and more accustomed to the words.

- Sing to them and read to them more often. Their introduction to language should not be through only one form, that is, talking. Let them listen to music so that the rhythm helps them ease into it.

- It becomes easier for kids to imitate you when you speak to them in a slightly high-pitched voice, using the typical "baby-talk" voice that we tend to use with kids. You can try that as well.

- In case you are still anxious, feel free to visit a doctor. But it is best to not panic or pressure your child unnecessarily.

Giving Your Child Potty Training

Potty training is as much a big deal for children as it is for parents. Remember the mantra- do not rush and have patience. It's going to be alright! Do not worry, for I am going to guide you through it now. Just follow the steps, and you and your baby should be good to go.

First things first- When to know that your baby is ready for the training? Here are some signs to look out for:

- Is your child able to walk or sit on a chair?

- Is your child able to pull up and pull down their pants by themselves?

- Can your child follow directions by themselves?

- Does your child manage to stay dry for two hours at a stretch?

If these signs are in place, your child is good to go. On average, between the age of 18 and 24, a child should be potty trained. Let me take you through some easy steps for that:

- You need to choose your words carefully. Make sure to not associate negative words like "dirty" or "bad" when you are training your child. Let them know that it is normal.

- Prepare the equipment well. Keep a potty chair in the washroom or the area where your child usually takes a dump. You need to encourage your child to sit on the potty chair while their feet are still touching the ground.

- Schedule the potty breaks carefully. The first thing in the morning and after they get up from their naps. Make sure you keep regular intervals. Your kid should start associating the potty breaks with the new arrangements.

- The next thing is to get there fast. Whenever you see that your child is showing signs of needing potty breaks or pee breaks, make sure to take them to the toilet immediately. They will eventually start associating the toilet with needing to relieve themselves.

- Ditch the diapers slowly. Do not hurry your child, but as they get more comfortable with the entire process, they won't need the diaper anymore.

- Teach them proper hygiene. They will take time to get used to this new process but make sure they flush the toilet themselves and wash their hands with soap after every toilet break. This will ease the process.

Teaching Your Toddler Discipline

One of the biggest concerns of every parent is to make sure that their child becomes disciplined and well-mannered. Kids can, at times, behave in ways that are not desirable, but when they learn the right way of behaving, they catch on really fast.

Remember that there is never a bad child, just bad behavior. So make sure you are starting right while teaching them the nuances of good behavior and discipline. Let's look at a few steps through which that can be achieved.

Focus on the Positives –

 Many a time, a child can misbehave to get your attention. It is not because they mean bad, but just because they don't know better.

While disciplining your kid, if you only focus on the negatives, they might get the wrong idea and use it in the future to get your attention. When you want to teach them what is right, then focus on the positives that they do. Let them understand what the better way to behave is.

Convey Your Expectations –

Convey transparently what you expect out of your child. Kids are very intelligent, and when you give them their deserved honesty, they will obviously act better.

Instead of scolding them all the time, talk like this "Kevin, I know you are a very responsible kid, and I do not expect this from you. Do not repeat it again, for I know you can do a lot better." When your child understands that you know they can do better, they will definitely behave better.

Explain the Consequences to Them –

Next time your child misbehaves, sit with your kid, and instead of shouting or getting angry, tell them what consequences their wrong deeds can bring.

Kids do not know what's at the end of their doings because they have no prior experience. But when you tell them the consequences, they will not repeat it again. "Kevin, if you go near the stove, the fire can harm you and others badly" will have a much better impact on the child rather than you cutting off their playtime.

Discipline in a Positive Manner –

Many parents have the misconception that raising their voice, showing angry faces, and keeping them away from things they like are effective ways to discipline a child when they misbehave. The reality is a bit different.

By taking an aggressive stance, you are only making your child more adamant about doing what they should not; simply because you are angry and scolding them does not make it clear to them about what they did wrong. You need to understand the difference between positive and negative discipline.

Schooling Your Child

Parents have a lot of dreams regarding their child's education and future. Schooling is one of the most crucial steps in a child's upbringing. But so is pre-schooling. As parents, if you plan it properly, easing your child into the entire educational process should not be difficult.

Children are like sponges, and they can instantly grasp all the new information they get. All you need to do is plan your child's education in a way that they have lots of fun in the way. Below, I am listing a few tips for you to do it with the least difficulty.

Develop a Home Curriculum –

At the beginning, make a list of everything your child should have an idea about before they start kindergarten.

Keep in mind to not cramp your child with information that they clearly do not need. Keep to the basics. When you have a list, it will be easier to help your child cover those bases.

Make it Fun –

Your child will be willing to learn if they are interested in that thing. Be it studies or extra-curricular. As long as a child is having fun, it will be easy to take that in.

You as parents have to make sure that learning is not becoming a burden. During the pre-schooling years, take help of music, different colored books, objects, and other things they like, to teach them. Do not make it monotonous.

Make it an All-Around Learning –

Remember that schooling your child is not restricted to studies. Your child needs to grow up with a stable and healthy emotional capacity as well to develop in an all-around manner.

The aim is not only growth but development. As parents, it is your duty to help your child learn manners, values, appropriate behavior.

That being said, I am listing below a few things that you can start with as far as pre-schooling is concerned.

- Start by helping your kid recognize the difference between various similar-looking objects. Say an eraser and a sharper. Teach them object differentiation.

- They should slowly learn how to sit at a place and listen to something, say music or a book-reading. This will increase their concentration power and help them understand things better.

- Give them ample pages and colors. Let them draw things that do not make sense. This is the time their individual perception is grown. They will try to replicate what they perceive in different things.

- As they progress a bit, start teaching them the basic alphabets. Use colorful books and even animated shows that are available. The audio-visual medium is very helpful in getting your child's attention.

- Tell them a story and let them ponder over it. Make the story interesting and answer all their questions. After some time, encourage them to retell the story. Say you had told them the story at dinner last night. During lunch the next morning, ask them to narrate the story to you.

- Go to writing next. As they become confident with memorizing the letters, teach them to write those. The best way is by showing them how their names look in writing. That is bound to get them excited.

- Teach them to label drawings and pictures. By now, they know what basic things are called, and they also know how to write simple words.

Having a child and raising them up is like reliving your childhood once again. Not only do you get to learn everything from the very beginning, but you also start seeing things from a whole new perspective.

Your child's first words, first steps, new ideas, food habits, quirks, different moods, everything is sure to take you through a rollercoaster of various emotions, which are both a treat and a cause of stress for parents. But at the end of the day, there is nothing as satisfying as seeing your child growing up happy and healthy.

I hope I was able to answer all your doubts through this chapter. As parents, you are always anxious to choose what is absolutely best for your child, and so even simple questions like "What will they eat?" or "When should they take a nap?" become huge concerns.

This chapter was aimed at answering some of the most commonly asked questions by parents, and I am sure that all the tips and tricks that I have mentioned will surely come to your aid. As parents, I know that you are giving your best in raising your child. Do not ever lose hope or get too anxious, for I promise you that things are going to be absolutely fine. I know that you will be able to raise a beautiful child. All my best wishes to you and your kid!

Exercise

Assign light work for your kid to do around the house.

What are your expectations from your kid in different areas? Write them down and make sure to convey these to them.

Write down ways in which you can make learning fun.

Chapter 5: Discipline

Your child is growing up, and with everything exciting and joyous that your child is bringing into your life, they are also adding a certain amount of stress. Why? Because their episodes of misbehavior are increasing. They are no more a kid who would listen to everything you tell them. It is only natural for you to worry and want to discipline your child.

The thing is, even if your child is not misbehaving too much or too often, disciplining them is required for them to be able to adjust to the society we live in. So let us get some basics clear first. What exactly do I mean by disciplining a child? Some might misinterpret it as rebuking or scolding a kid when they do something wrong.

While it is true that you need to scold a child at times when they do something wrong, disciplining them is a more inclusive idea. It is where you, as parents, teach them the correct ways of behavior and mannerisms that are acceptable to society.

You help them choose right from wrong, and you prepare them to develop into responsible human beings. It includes verbal, non-verbal, audio-visual aids, and much more, through which a child can learn and thus be disciplined. In this chapter, I will take you through some of those ways in which you can discipline your child without getting tangled in a needless power struggle with them.

Discipline Your Child Non-Verbally

Body language alone can be a great medium of conveying to your child that they are not supposed to do what they are doing. You will not even need words, leave alone yelling, to let your child understand that you do not appreciate a certain kind of behavior. I will give you a few simple tips for this. Next time your child does something they are not supposed to, try these and see the difference.

Reveal the Power of Eye-Contact –

I am sure there have been times when you have felt your words are having absolutely no impact on your child, and you are talking to a wall. Well, why not change it and make them aware of their fault some other way! When you see they are doing something wrong, say touching things without asking for permission in someone else's house, then do not say a single word. Just look at them intently and nod your head sideways.

Kids are intelligent, and they will take the hint immediately. They are growing up and developing a sense of the self. They definitely do not want to be humiliated. They will see the look in your eyes and immediately keep what they were touching.

Let Your Hands Talk –

Let me get this straight. By using your hands, I definitely don't mean hitting anyone. NO! Instead, go and place your hands over there's, stopping them from doing what they were doing.

Say you have taken your kid for a birthday party. You see them snatching a toy from another kid. The first instinct is to shout at them and take that toy away. The moment you do that, they are going to cry and engage in a psychological power struggle, creating a mess. You don't want that in front of everyone. So go and touch their arm. The moment they look at you and your hands, they will get the hint. The same thing will not be repeated again.

Go Near Them –

 Sometimes, just walking near them does the trick. Say you see from far that they are about to create trouble. Imagine you have told them to finish their homework, and you see they are playing under their chair.

You need not even say or do anything. They are doing that because they think you cannot see it. Just start walking towards them. The moment they realize you have noticed them, they are going to get back to their work. When you see them getting back to their homework, just walk past them as if nothing has happened. They will get the hint, and your work will be done.

The idea is to convey to your child what they ought and ought not to do. It does not matter what way you choose as long as the results are coming. When you can discipline them without shouting or yelling, why not take advantage of that, right!

Discipline Your Kid with Narratives

Narratives, that is, drama or stories, have been an age-old method of teaching kids many important values and disciplining them. If you take notice, every cartoon they watch, every story they read, has a moral at the end. Their purpose is to get your kid's attention through colorful audio-visual means and teach them something important in the process.

Why do they work? Because they teach your kids in a language, they understand. You have to apply the same. Discipline your kids in a way they understand. In most cases, your child is not listening to you because they do not understand what you mean. So what can you do? You can tell stories that will help them get the message. Let's see how.

Do it When They Are Calm –

Your child will hardly understand what you are trying to tell them when they are upset. It's the same with us, right? We understand better when we are calm. So after the episode of a tantrum has passed and your child is calm, choose such a time to tell them the story that you want.

Fabricate the story to focus on the message that you want to tell them. Revolve the story around their favorite characters to get them more engaged. They will not only enjoy the story but also understand what you are trying to say because they are calm and happy.

Make Sure They Have Fun –

You know, I had this math teacher at school who used to make our classes full of fun and laughter just because she knew many of us were scared of that subject. Surprisingly, things used to make more sense in her classes because we were having fun.

Children will always understand better when they are having fun. It is true that they have made a mistake, and you are upset with them. But no matter how much you try, they will not realize their mistake while they are crying because you have scolded them.

Stories will have the opposite impact. Make the story as fun as possible so that they can enjoy it. At the same time, when you are teaching them something, make them as comfortable as you can. The message will hit home when it sounds like a friendly conversation and not a dictum.

Ask Them Their Opinion –

As adults, I am sure you already know how reverse psychology works, right? You make your target come to the conclusions themselves without giving them any answers. That is exactly what you need to do with kids. As you are telling them a story or showing them any drama that has the desired message, ask them questions constantly.

"Why do you think he did not take that toy without permission?" "why do you think she listened to her teacher?" "why do you think she let her sister have that ice cream?" Questions like these will help your child think and come to the correct conclusions by themselves. Neither will they feel pressured, nor will they feel challenged. It will be their favorite characters doing something and them understanding the correct thing through that narrative.

What to do if Your Child is Throwing a Fit

Your toddler is throwing a tantrum in spite of you telling them otherwise. What do you do? You start questioning your parenting abilities. You might feel there is something seriously wrong with how you are teaching your kid. Let me tell you how wrong you are. Throwing tantrums has got nothing to do with your parenting skills. It is an extremely normal part of being a toddler.

The natural instinct is to get angry and irritated and react in a negative manner. But do you know how this behavior of yours replays to your child? Them throwing a tantrum is normal to them, so when they find no fault in their action, you scolding them replays as YOU throwing a tantrum.

Children do not understand that. I am suggesting a few simple steps to follow next time your child is having a fit and needs to be disciplined.

Do Not Yell –

Always remember that you are your child's role model. You cannot afford to put up with any such behavior that you do not want your child to take on. Yelling is one of them. You are stressed, but yelling will neither lessen your stress nor discipline your child. So refrain from yelling. Your child is growing up and starting to develop their own character.

The moment you yell, there starts a power struggle which can make them more adamant. So take a few deep breaths and handle the situation calmly. Let your child see that any adverse situation can be handled without yelling or throwing tantrums. That itself will be a lesson. Also, your child is throwing a tantrum because they have their reasons for it. Try to get to that problem first instead of yelling. The faster you reach that, the faster they will stop.

Stop Them from Getting Aggressive –

One thing, however, that they need to understand immediately is that aggression of any sort is NOT acceptable. In case you see that your child is getting aggressive, be it hitting or kicking others, remove them from the spot immediately. For them to understand their mistake clearly, take away their toys for some time or do not let them watch their cartoons for a few days, or remove any other privilege that they get for some time.

A strict message should reach them that being aggressive is not permitted. That being said, analyze the entire situation. It could be that your child was provoked to do that by someone, or maybe they are having some discomfort in their body. Do not punish them unnecessarily. Know what has happened and then make decisions.

Ignore it if Possible –

I have already mentioned this in previous chapter. Ignoring can be a useful tool for disciplining your child. They throw tantrums at times just to get your attention. When you pretend that you are not bothered, given that what they have done is really minor, they will take the hint and not repeat it.

When they see that tantrums are not bringing them their desired result, they will automatically stop after a point. You ignoring them will indicate you do not appreciate what they are doing, and that itself will discipline them.

Help Your Child to Gain Self-Confidence

It falls on you to see that your child grows up knowing their worth – that they learn to identify their powers and rectify their mistakes. You, as parents, should be the first ones to celebrate the goodness in them and, above all, help them realize that they can do anything if they want.

It is normal for a child to feel inhibited at times simply because they are not yet aware of their potential. You need to help them tap into their power resource and develop self-confidence in them. Here are a few tips for you to help your child with self confidence.

Let Them Identify the Problem –

A lot of times, children face difficulties in handling something because they fear the unknown. The world is new to them, and they do not know what to expect. Instead of dictating it to them, let your child identify the problem.

"Why don't you want to go to soccer practice? Did someone tell you anything or you don't like the sport?" It could be because some other kid has told them something and not because they don't like the sport. When they find out the problem themselves, they will get a lot more confidence to deal with it.

Let Them Be Curious –

 Never stop your kid from being curious. The more they want to know, the better. Some parents get irritated and don't encourage questions. But the more they know, the clearer their ideas are going to be. This is a great way to boost a child's self-confidence.

Do not ever stunt their curiosity. Let them explore and help them get in control. Say they are showing curiosity about a certain sport. Make sure you sit with them and explain the game, the pros, and the cons. Now when they start the sport, they will perform much better, given they already know what is in store.

Appreciate Whether They Win or Lose –

I know you appreciate your kid's achievements. But it is equally important to appreciate when they lose. I will tell you why. The moment they lose, it is natural for them to start doubting themselves.

But if they see that their parents are beside them, supporting them through thick and thin, they will not be afraid to try the next time again. Their self-confidence will increase a lot when they understand that it is okay to lose—participating matters the most. As parents, help them to learn from their mistakes instead of criticizing them.

Discipline in the Correct Way

So far, I have talked at length about discipline and the different ways in which you can implement that. But now comes the most important question. "How can you discipline your child in a way that makes sense?" It is crucial to know what are the things that you should not practice in the name of discipline.

One of the reasons your child is not listening to you is probably because your way of disciplining them is probably not making sense to them. So make sure you are applying age-appropriate methods to discipline your kid to get the best results. Here are a few points that you should keep in mind.

Set Achievable Limits and Stick to Them –

Did you know that kids thrive when they have a structured life? By that, I do not mean they need to live a prison life with hundreds of rules and with fear of strict punishments. What I mean is, you know best what values you want them to imbibe and what is important for your family and their growing up. So, make sure that all the boxes are checked, and make a routine for them to follow.

Set achievable limits for them and encourage them towards it. They should feel excited and interested. When they see that they have a positive environment that allows them to grow, they will definitely prosper. Let them also know that misbehavior is not appreciated so that they do not get distracted. Not through yelling or something aggressive, but when you tell them what results await them at the end of misbehavior, they will give more effort to doing the work better.

Give Them Positive Attention –

Children need attention, and that is a fact. When elders do not give them the attention they need, kids tend to astray and resort to tantrums or other negative modes of gaining attention. So do not think that if they misbehave, not giving them the attention will teach them a lesson. Well, that will not happen. You need to know what is bothering your kid to help them behave properly.

So make sure you are filling them up with positive attention. Scolding them, yelling at them, and taking away their toys are all ways of "disciplining" a child, but they are the causes of negative attention. Refrain from practicing those.

You could try reading their favorite book or playing their favorite game. The aim is to let your kid realize that you care about their needs, likes, and dislikes. That way, they will feel loved, cared, and not neglected. They won't have the additional need for seeing attention anymore then. That's the aim.

Give Them Time for Training –

Know for a fact that teaching a child anything takes time, and you need to have patience. When you train them over a long period of time, they do not feel hurried or under any pressure. They get time to learn better without any inhibitions. As parents, your aim should be to help them get a grip on things around them.

So if you see your child is having trouble learning something, don't hurry them. It is probably because they are not ready. Give them time and let them know that you are there. Disciplining your child will only have any sense when your child understands properly what they are doing wrong and how they can improve.

I hope you are worrying a little less now. Now that you have understood the various ways you can help your child develop beautifully, I am sure that you are at emotional ease as parents. I get your concern completely because, at the end of the day, all of us are trying our best to provide the best for our kids. But it is not easy for them as well, isn't it? As adults, we are already trained to behave in a certain way and make our decisions.

But this world is new to our kids. They are just starting out. They need to have the freedom to make their mistakes as well as to learn. Rest assured, you are always there to catch them if they fall. So do not worry about disciplining your child. Enjoy them as much as you can because, trust me, they are going to grow up so soon, and then you will miss these childish tantrums.

Exercise

Create a few narratives for disciplining your child in a fun way.

____

____

____

____

____

____

____

____

____

____

____

____

____

Chapter 6: Putting Toddlerhood in Context

A new phase of development in a child begins the moment they begin taking their first steps. It gives them the freedom to roam about their world, and they begin to explore the environment around them. Their language development happens in leaps at this stage. You will notice that your toddler begins to learn names of things they like and even asks for things.

They begin to have a say in things, which means they also develop the ability to say no. Psychologists say that the major challenge for parents is to regulate their child's emotions at this stage. Meltdowns at this stage of development are common. This is the age they learn to actively say no, but they also need to learn to accept the 'no' from others. Your child may refuse to listen to you and may begin to misbehave when their demands are not fulfilled.

Dealing with tantrums on a daily basis can be a challenge, and you may lean towards inflicting corporal punishment when you lose your patience, but that is illegal if you know. So, how do you deal with tantrums? You will need to make use of the bond that you developed with your child during infancy to help them learn to modulate their emotional expression and be habituated with the concept of delayed gratification. How can you do that? The first thing you would need to do is have a little more patience and incorporate some of the tools and techniques mentioned below in your parenting techniques.

What Tools Can You Use to Control Tantrums?

Seeing your calm and polite child suddenly turn into a monster, stomping and screaming when their demands are not met, can generate anxiety in you as a parent. Remember that tantrums in kids aged 2-4 are common, and your child is no different. Before you move to learn ways to control tantrums, understand why it happens.

When your child throws a tantrum, their intention is not to embarrass you or frustrate you. Toddlers begin to develop a sense of self which makes them want to do things themselves. They are not fully skilled to ask clearly for what they want, and this gap between what they desire and their ability to do so can cause them to be frustrated, which takes the shape of meltdowns, tantrums, and unruly behavior. To cope with such episodes of frustration, you have to –

Notice the triggers –

When does your child throw a tantrum? Hunger, sleep, tiredness, and boredom can be reasons for your child to throw tantrums. They may also do so when they are sick or their parent's attention is diverted from them. Notice what triggers such behavior as anticipation can be useful in preventing tantrums.

When you know what can cause them to throw a fit, you can redirect them with other choices so that the tantrum ensues.

For instance, when you take your child to the store with you, talk to them beforehand that they are not allowed to eat candies. But, if they behave well, then they would get a treat for it. Give them the opportunity to make such small choices often.

Maintain your calm and try to ignore –

This is definitely not easy to do when your child is bringing your house down but try to be patient as long as you can. If you turn aggressive or shout, your child will try to match your volume. Your calmness can help them cool off and subside their frustration.

For instance, your child is kicking, hitting, or doing something that would put both their and others safety in danger. You, however, cannot sit idly in this situation. Hug them or gently place your hands on their shoulders. Calming physical presence without speaking can also be effective.

Let your child be angry –

Just like you need to vent to get your anger out, your child needs to do the same. You just have to be careful that the process involves nothing that can hurt them. This will be helpful for them to get their feelings out.

It will also allow them to gain back control over themselves and pull themselves together without engaging in a battle of wills or yelling match with you. Sometimes give in to their demands but not unreasonably. For example, tell your child that you will allow them to snack on a candy bar if they stop crying.

Create a distraction –

A child's attention span is short, which is why it is easy to divert their minds. If your child has been asking too long for the frosted cereal and you think they can throw a tantrum if you blatantly say no, try to take their attention away from it.

Ask them to help you pick a flavor of ice cream or come see the big lobsters in the tank.

Help your child get rid of frustration –

Your child may be crying because they are unable to tie and wear their shoes correctly. Help them with the task so that they may have a sense of accomplishment.

Sometimes they may want to climb a ladder, but that can be unsafe. In such a situation, firmly state that it can be risky. To soothe this sudden adventurous spirit, give them an alternative too. Tell them that you will take them to the park where they can instead climb the slide ladder.

What Tools Can You Use to Correct Everyday Misbehavior?

When your two-year-old screams for chocolates and begins to throw items out of your shopping cart at the supermarket, you may find it hard to come up with a way to stop this misbehavior. You may think that they are too young to be disciplined, but actually, it is not true.

Most parents think that disciplining their child would involve punishment, but this is not the case. They may be too young to understand cause and effect, but this can be the right time to teach them right and wrong. You can set your toddler on the right path by using the following strategies –

Listen carefully –

Your child will feel better when they know that they have been heard. So, whenever it is possible, repeat the concerns of your child. Let us again take the grocery store example where your child is upset because you would not allow them to open the packet of chips.

Tell them that you are aware of how badly they want to eat the chips, but you cannot give them permission for it as you cannot use things from the store until you have paid for them. Such words are simple to say, and they may not satisfy your child's urge but at least will reduce the chances of them conflicting and misbehaving.

Explain the rules to your child –

When you say no to something, your child will likely be adamant and will continue to ask for it until they have been satisfied. They will not stop doing something that seems fun to them just because you have asked them to stop.

For instance, your child snatches the toy of their playmate because they like it. Tell them that their action would hurt their friend. Help your child see what consequences their actions may have and how they can directly affect other people.

Give them choices –

Sometimes, parents think that being strict is the best way to discipline children, and giving them choices may spoil them. It is not true. When your child refuses to do something, the real issue behind it is - control. You, as a parent, have got the control, but they want it. Then, does giving choices mean losing your control?

No, because you are the one who will offer them a limited set of choices. For example, if you ask your child to pick up their books, they may not want to do it. Instead, ask them if they want to pick up their books first or their toys. It gives them the freedom to choose their action at the same time you are in control of the situation. Give them some control whenever possible by giving them such choices.

Provide them alternatives –

For instance, your child is banging with a toy hammer, and you want them to stop doing it. Give them an alternative that would help them express their emotions which they were doing through the previous action. Giving them alternatives will help them learn that their behavior or form of expression is unacceptable.

Also, give your child the freedom to come up with their own solutions. Say they are upset over their friend not sharing their toys with your child. Ask your child what they can do so that their friend would share the toys with them. Listen to their ideas with a clear mind without shooting down anything. Try to talk about the consequences with them before arriving at a decision.

Use time-out –

For moments when reasoning, if none of the above seem to work, use time-outs. Ask your child to sit at a corner and pull themselves together.

It will give you a chance to cool down and, at the same time, will get the message across to them that they cannot win your attention with negative behavior.

If you stop giving attention to negative behaviour, your child will use it less to get what they want.

Give them rewards –

The truth is that your child will not always do what you ask them to do. Make judicious use of treats. Shower them with love and rewards when they behave appropriately.

Such positive enforcements will motivate them to behave well and, at the same time, will give credibility to your discipline demands.

How to Sculpt Your Toddler's Behavior Using Stories and Drama?

It might sound like a dream, but in reality, it is possible to shape your child's behavior through storytelling or using narratives. It is also called Inuit parenting. Anger and yelling do not find a place in Inuit parenting.

Storytelling is a part of Inuit parenting, and the indigenous people of the Arctic use it skillfully to sculpt their children's behavior. For instance, if their child, despite warning several times, goes near the sea, they would ideally start relaying the story of a monster who is notorious for jumping up and grabbing children by their feet who come too close to the sea.

You, too, in a similar way, can incorporate folklores or stories in your parenting techniques to make a point to your child. You might think that America does not have too many folklores that can be used, but you can still incorporate this method into your parenting style.

You can employ your strategy depending on your beliefs. Monsters do not exist in reality, and when you tell your child about them, it is a useful tool to caution your child from something dangerous.

This method of parenting also can be used to teach children to be responsible. Reasoning and nagging do not work with all children, and creative approaches such as this can still help you achieve your parenting goals without losing your calm.

What Are Some Specific Problem Behaviors in Toddlers and How Can You Solve Them?

Behavioral issues at the age of two to four are terrible. Although it is a part of growing up, ignoring such problems can become a habit and take bigger shape later in life. But, these problems are mostly temporary and eventually disappear as the child begins to grow up. You can, as a parent, manage the specific behavioral issues children have at this stage through some very easy solutions.

Temper tantrums –

Your kid is expected to be exposed to a wide range of emotions at this age. They may not be able to express themselves clearly but can understand most of what you say. This sometimes can be frustrating for your child and can lead to temper tantrums. Your child, during such an episode, may throw things, scream, or cry loudly.

The solution is simple – remain calm. Things could go west if you shout and raise your voice. Get down to the eye level of your child and hold their hand. Pick them up or hug them. Let them know that you love them and all will be well. If the tantrum still continues, let them vent out, and once they have calmed down, you can explain things to them.

Aggressive behavior –

Not knowing how to handle feelings in an appropriate manner can be the cause of aggression in your child.

Whenever your child shows aggression, give them an immediate consequence. Take away privileges.

Behavior problem in the car –

 Toddlers filled with energy find it difficult to sit for long hours in the car, and you can expect some tantrums during your journey.

Talk to your child beforehand about the car journey. Establish rules for food and pee breaks. Keep toys handy in the car that will keep them busy. Speak to them at consistent intervals to ensure all is well.

Mealtime behavior –

Your child could either be a picky eater or may claim to be hungry every half an hour. They may even sneak snacks that they are not permitted to eat. Remember that any food-related behavior can later become a power struggle for your child or give rise to body image issues, so you must handle them carefully.

Make your child understand that food is a necessity that keeps one alive and energetic; it is not entertainment for when they are bored. You cannot take the same approach if your child throws away the vegetables. If you tell them veggies are good for health, they are still going to refuse to eat them as common psychology among children is that healthy food tastes bad. Instead, tell them how vegetables can be delicious too.

Bedtime and sleep problems –

Bedtime challenges are again common. Your child may want to sleep with you or refuse to stay in bed. Not sleeping at the right time can leave your child sleep-deprived, and lack of sleep has been proven to increase behavioral problems in children.

Make sure that you are actively promoting healthy sleep habits. Establish bedtime rules, and here, consistency is the key. Even if you have to send back your child a dozen times to their bed, do it.

Lying –

A child at this age is unlikely to be able to differentiate between reality and fantasy. Lying as a concept is still unknown to them; they do not even know what truth means. Children at this age have an active imagination, so they often create imaginary creatures or friends and can deny having spilled the milk or drawing on the wall.

The way you accuse adults of doing something will not work in the case of your toddler. You will have to create an environment of trust and promote a dialogue where it will be easier for them to confess the truth.

Dressing problems –

Trying to get your toddler to stand still for dressing them or diapering them is a challenge in itself, and if you spend more time every morning dressing your child than yourself, you need to check this fussy behavior.

Let your child choose what to wear as when you give choices, they become less combative. Any clothes you would not want them to wear, keep them out of sight. If your child begins to fuss when you put the sweater over their head, talk to them about something that would draw their attention away from the dressing.

Sibling rivalry –

Most children like undivided attention. They are dependent on you for love, care, and affection at this age. Sometimes they may view a sibling as someone who would take away the attention of the parents from them.

As a parent, you have a big role to play here. Ensure that you dedicate quality alone time to all your children. Teach them the difference between equal and fair, that because of the age differences, they have different roles and responsibilities. Also, praise them when they get along well.

Behavior problems at preschool/school –

Disruptive talking in classrooms, fighting with peers, and name-calling at the playground are some behavior problems children demonstrate at preschool/schools.

As a parent, try to assess the situation. Engage with their teacher and therapist to find out how and why they have been behaving this way. Find out if they are being teased or not being looked after by their teacher. Talking with the teacher can help you come up with a solution. It is also wise to give your child a break sometimes. Give them a day off from school and engage in an activity they like to do.

Apart from the above-mentioned specific problems, there are other behavioral problems too that are common among toddlers –

Whining –

Your child may take this route to get what they want, and it can be a bad habit. How can you handle it? At first, try to ignore it, which will show that this tactic of theirs cannot change your mind. Give them attention only when they stop whining. You can teach them healthy ways to express their feelings. For instance, instead of whining when not taken to the park, teach them to express their sadness for the same.

Screaming –

Your child may not always scream when they are angry. Probably they are full of energy, or they do it because you run to them every time; they get your attention as a result. Teach your child the difference between a soft and a loud voice and make it clear they will be heard only when they speak softly.

Kicking and biting –

This is another way children show aggression. Shouting and scolding may not be effective, so instead, assign a naughty chair in the house and put them up on it if they show such behavior and do not bring them down till they have calmed down.

Using common sense instead of force will take you a long way when it comes to sculpting your toddler's behavior. Understand that such behavior could be a result of their exposure to the new things around them.
However, the earlier these problems are handled, the better, or else they may carry these issues into their childhood and adulthood.

Now that you have reached the end of this book, let's hope it was useful to you. I would be extremely grateful if you could leave a review on Amazon.

Exercise

Note down the trigger that causes your child to throw a tantrum. Knowing the triggers can help prevent tantrums.

ONE LAST THING

If you enjoyed this book or found it helpful. Please help us by writing a short review on Amazon. Your support makes a difference, and I read your reviews personally. So I can get your feedback and make this book even better.

To leave a review, you must go to amazon and type Parenting Toddlers by Trista frost. Click on the book; you will find the review option at the bottom of the page.

Thanks a lot for your support.